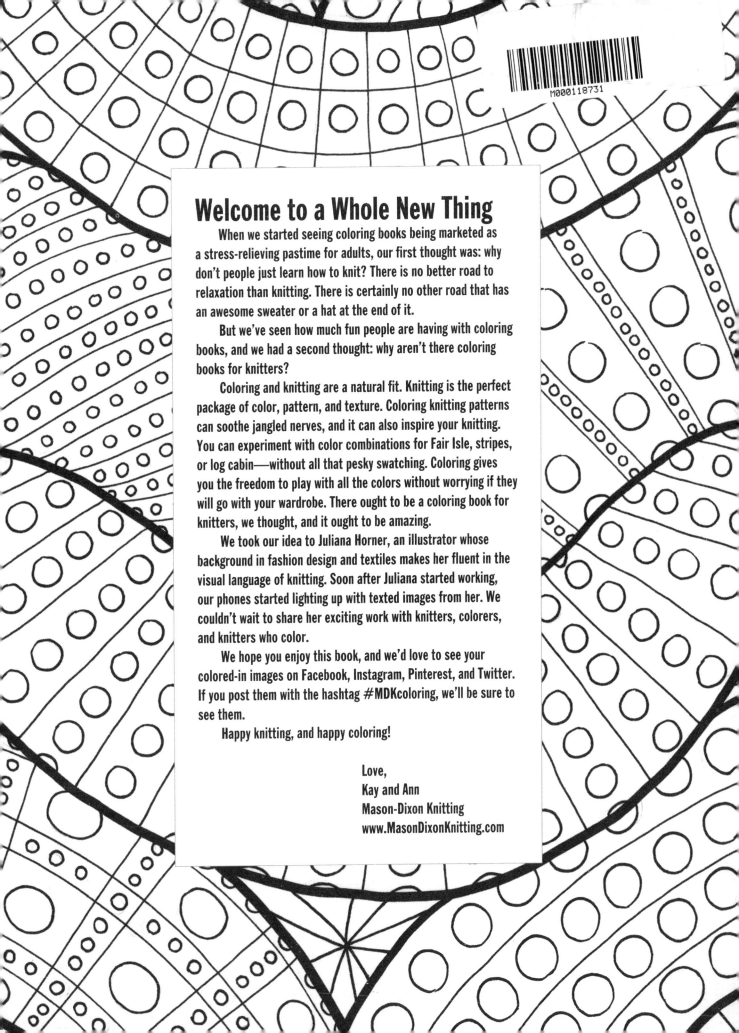

Welcome to a Whole New Thing

When we started seeing coloring books being marketed as a stress-relieving pastime for adults, our first thought was: why don't people just learn how to knit? There is no better road to relaxation than knitting. There is certainly no other road that has an awesome sweater or a hat at the end of it.

But we've seen how much fun people are having with coloring books, and we had a second thought: why aren't there coloring books for knitters?

Coloring and knitting are a natural fit. Knitting is the perfect package of color, pattern, and texture. Coloring knitting patterns can soothe jangled nerves, and it can also inspire your knitting. You can experiment with color combinations for Fair Isle, stripes, or log cabin—without all that pesky swatching. Coloring gives you the freedom to play with all the colors without worrying if they will go with your wardrobe. There ought to be a coloring book for knitters, we thought, and it ought to be amazing.

We took our idea to Juliana Horner, an illustrator whose background in fashion design and textiles makes her fluent in the visual language of knitting. Soon after Juliana started working, our phones started lighting up with texted images from her. We couldn't wait to share her exciting work with knitters, colorers, and knitters who color.

We hope you enjoy this book, and we'd love to see your colored-in images on Facebook, Instagram, Pinterest, and Twitter. If you post them with the hashtag #MDKcoloring, we'll be sure to see them.

Happy knitting, and happy coloring!

Love,
Kay and Ann
Mason-Dixon Knitting
www.MasonDixonKnitting.com

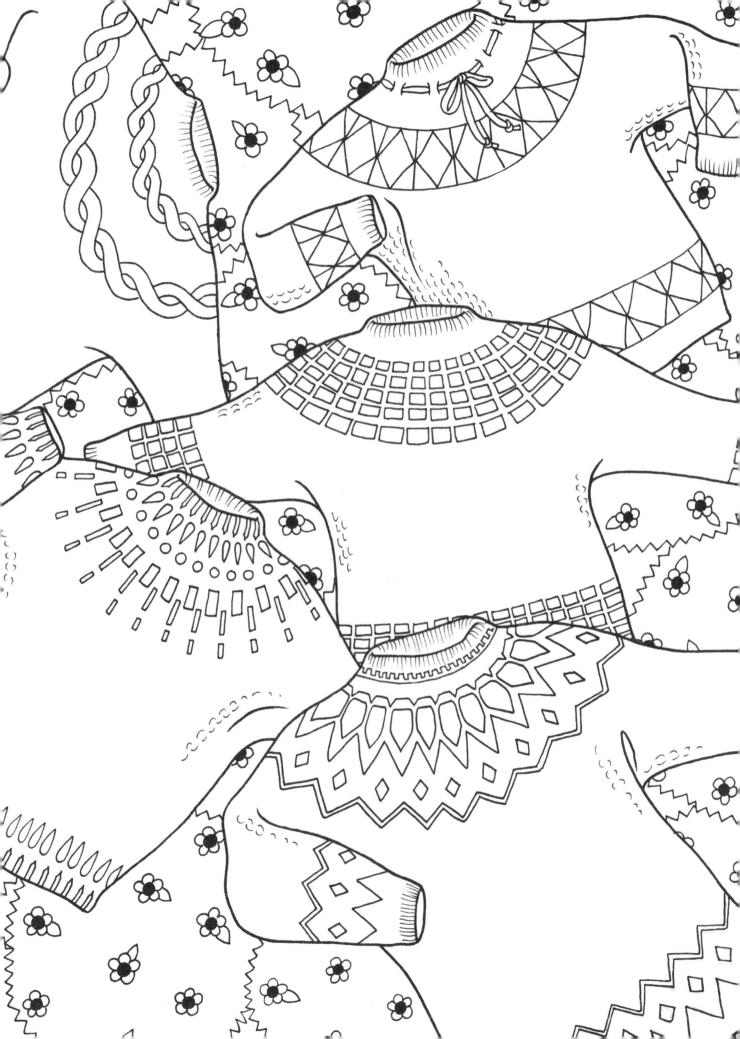

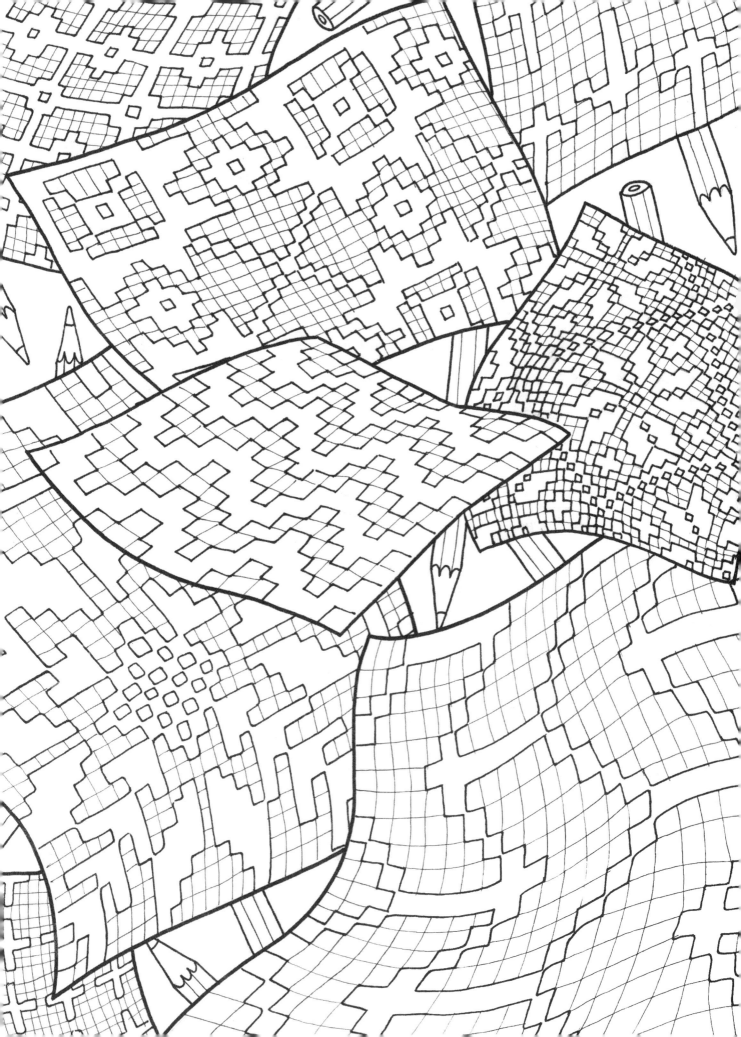

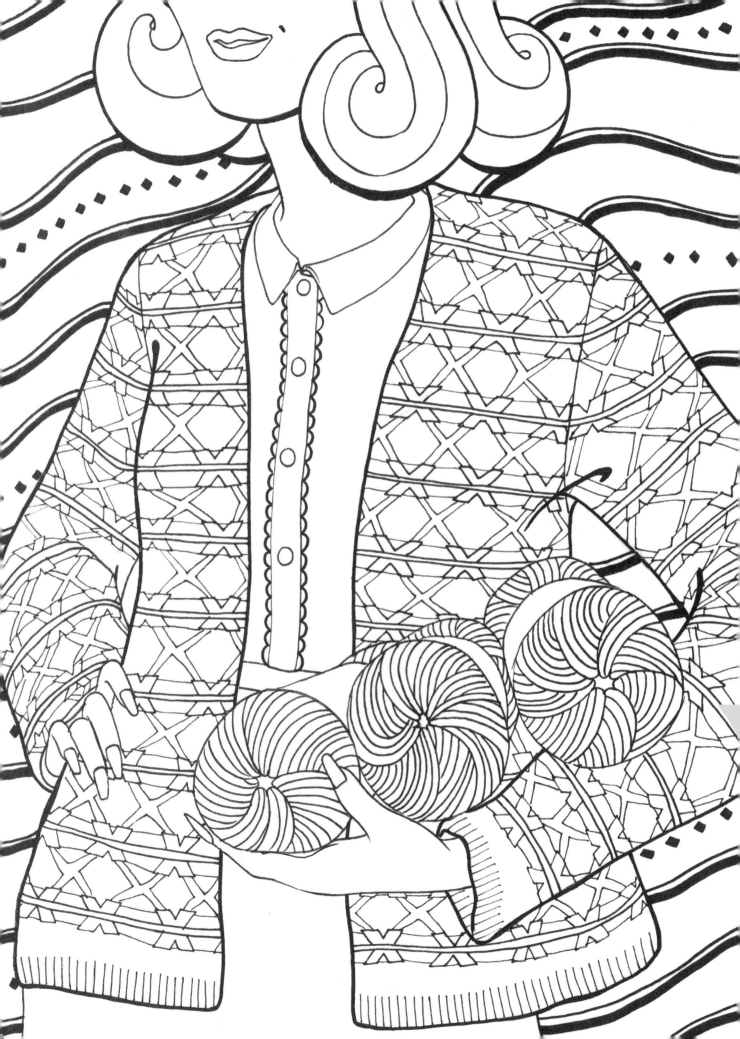

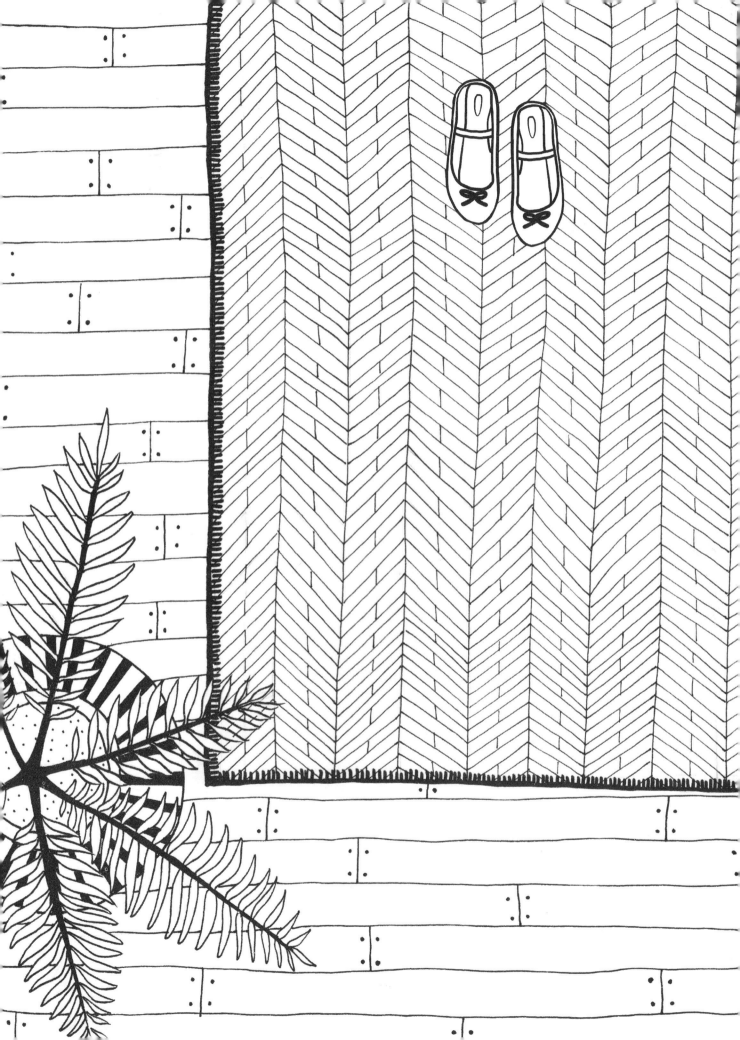

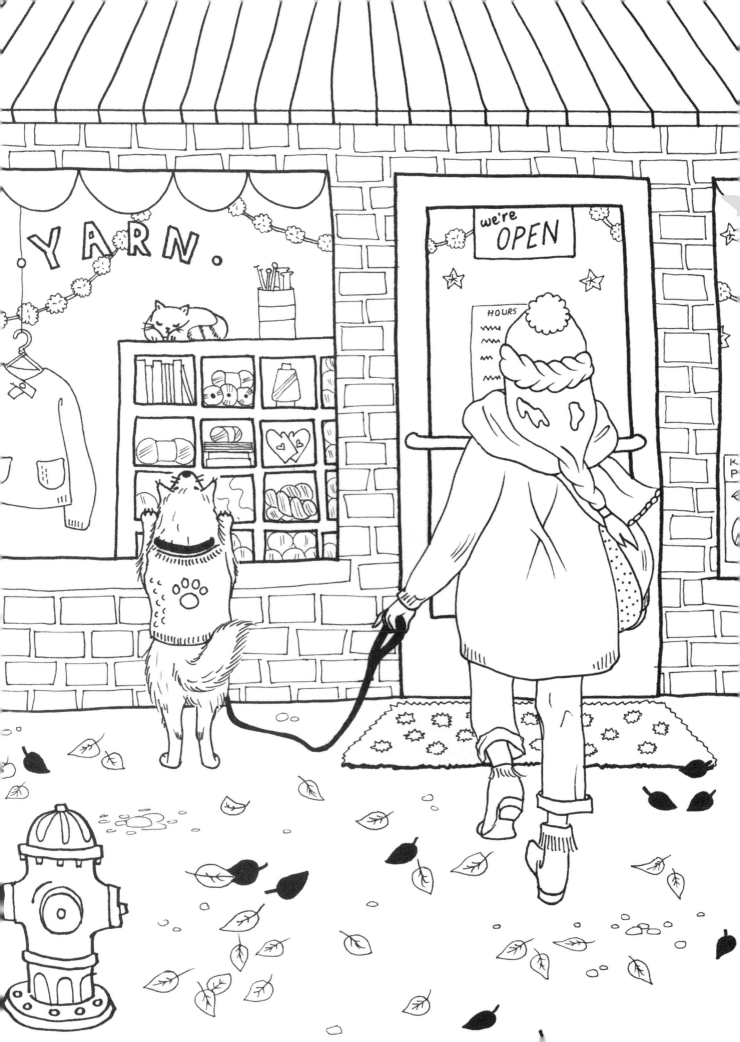

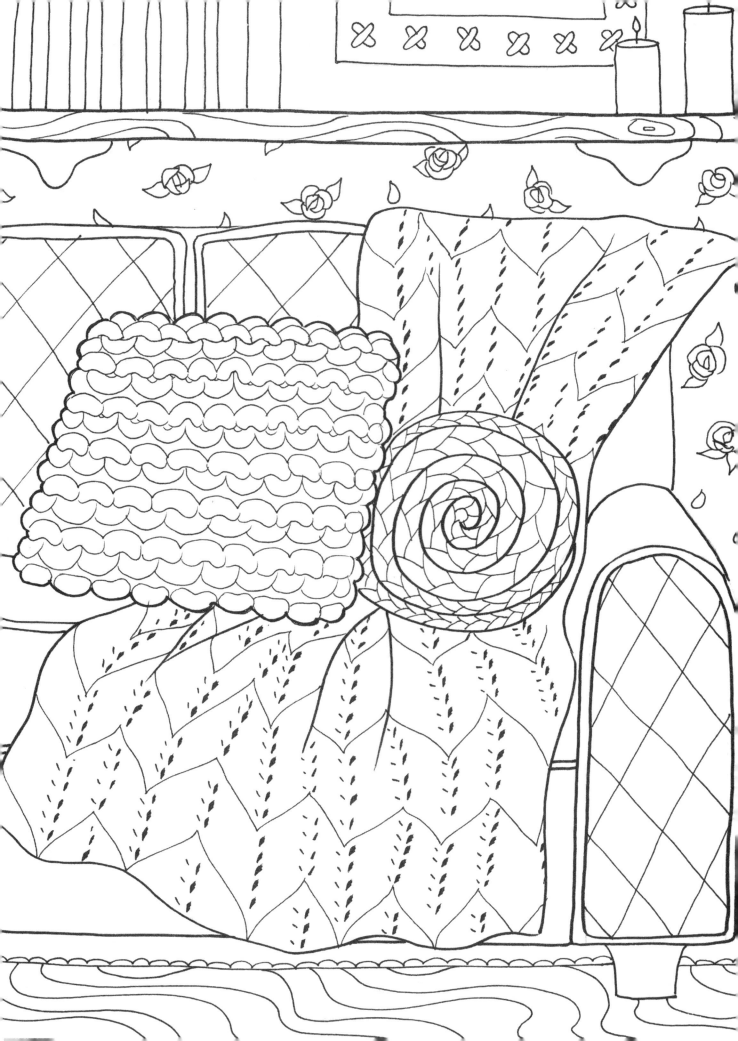

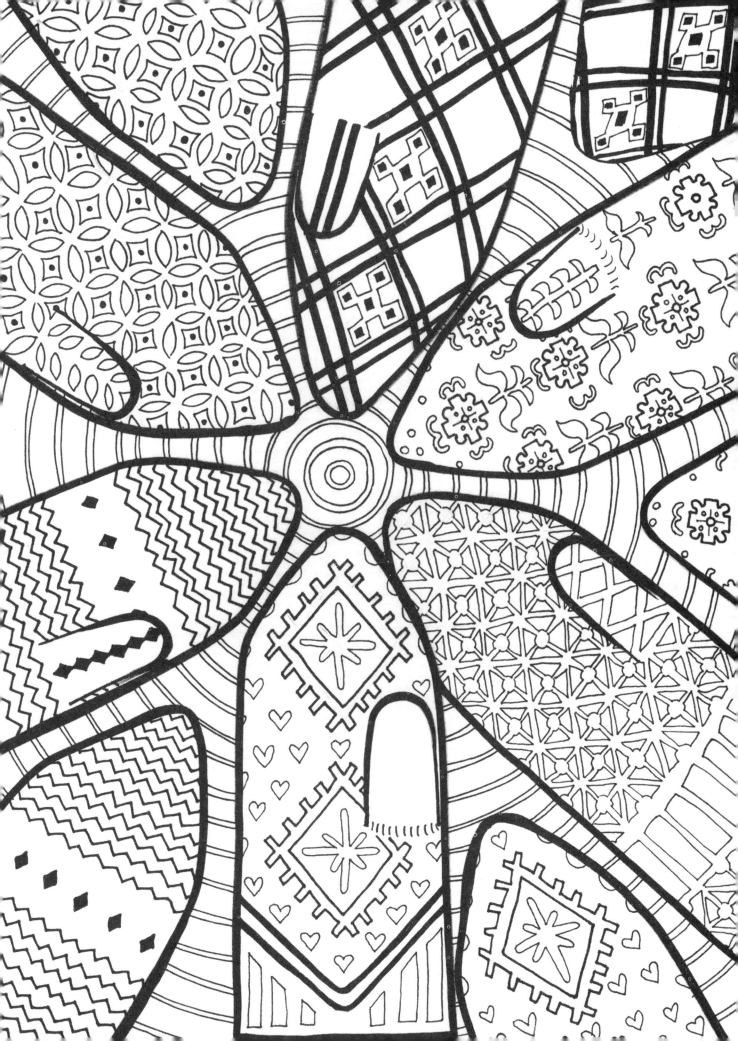

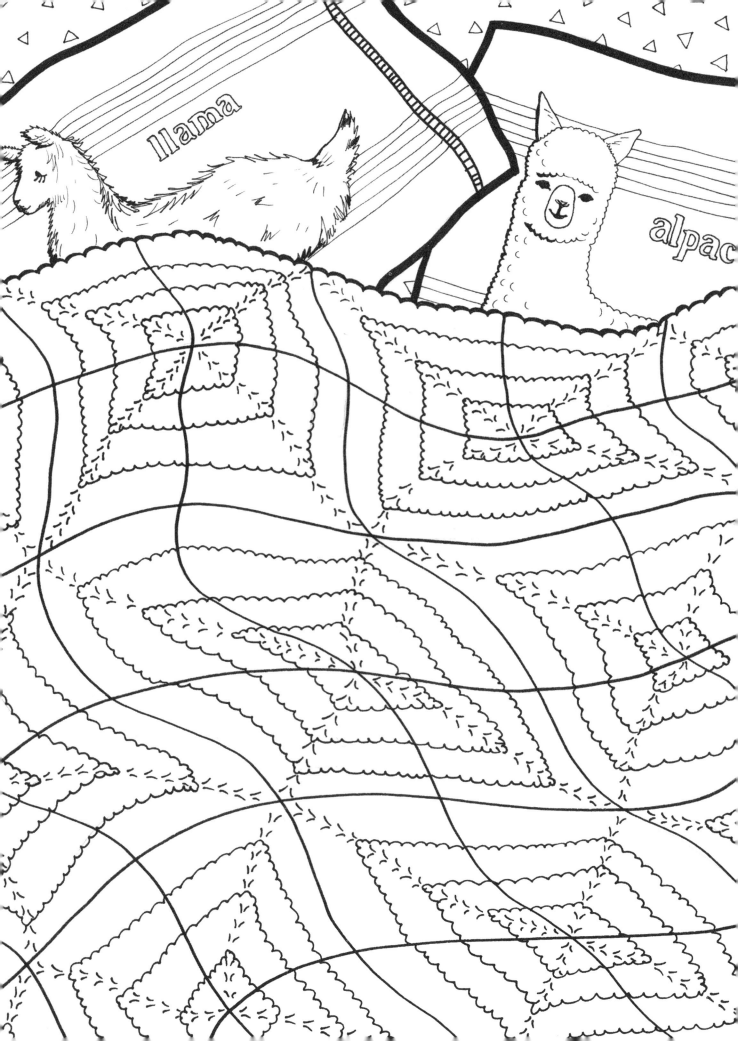

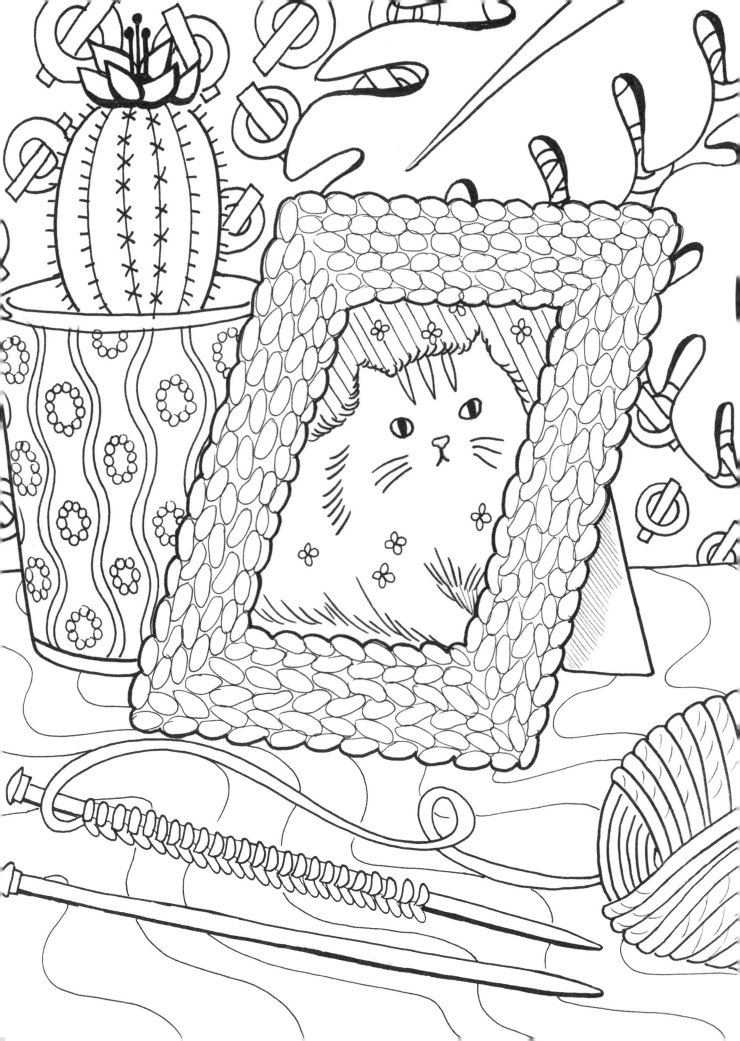

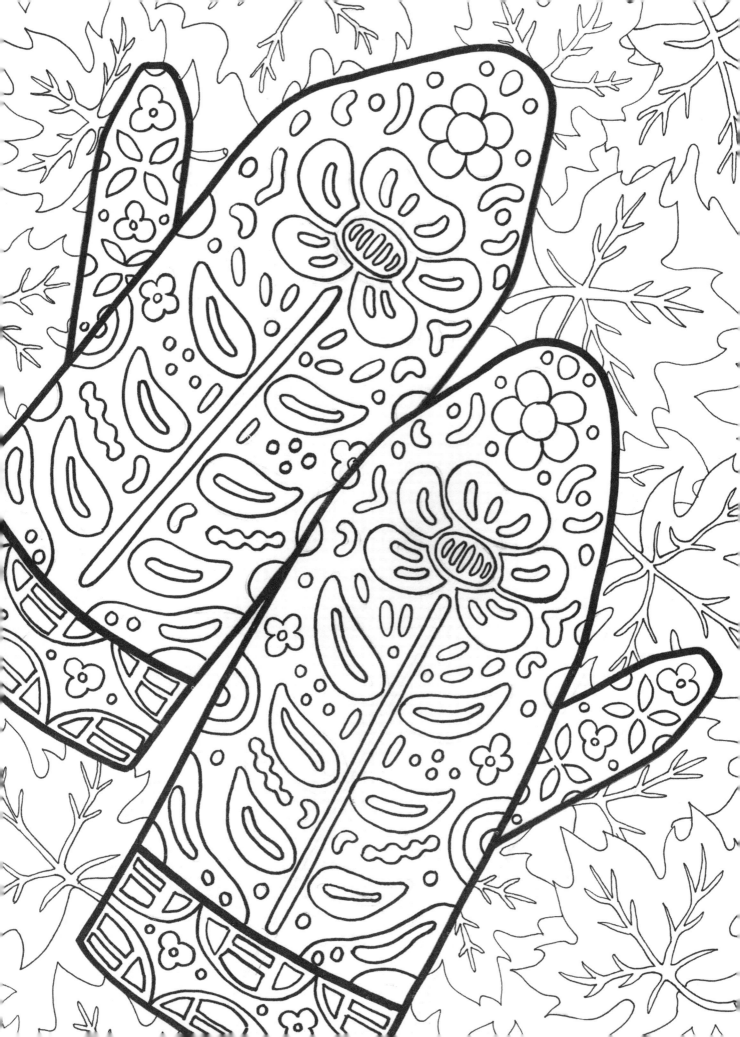

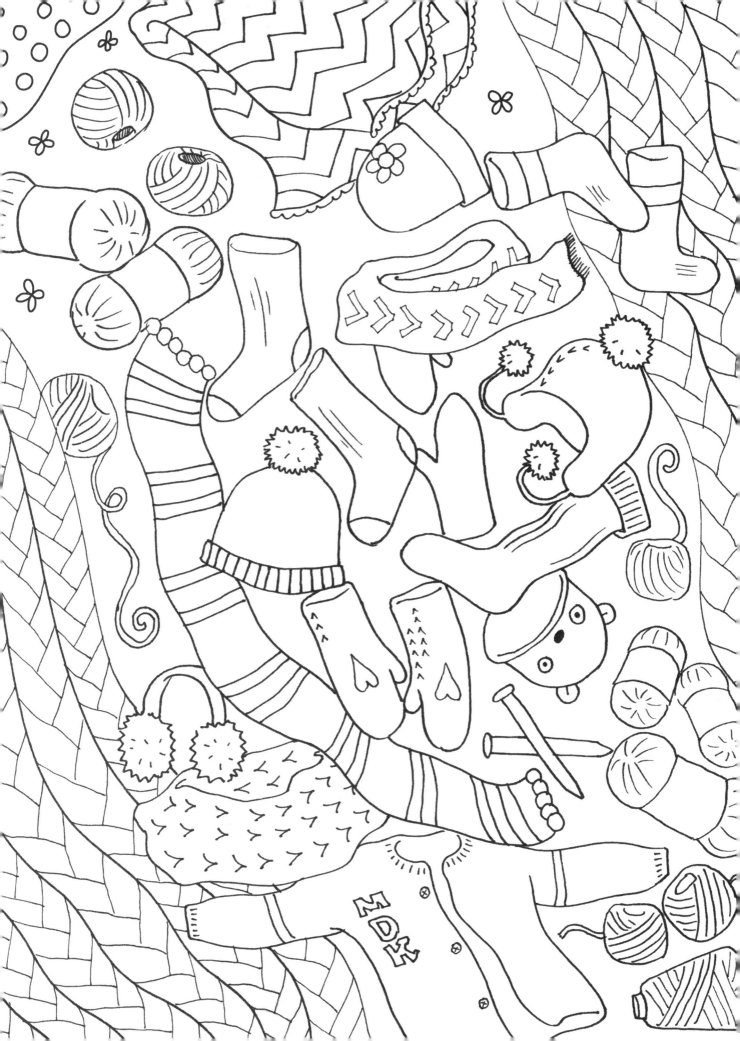

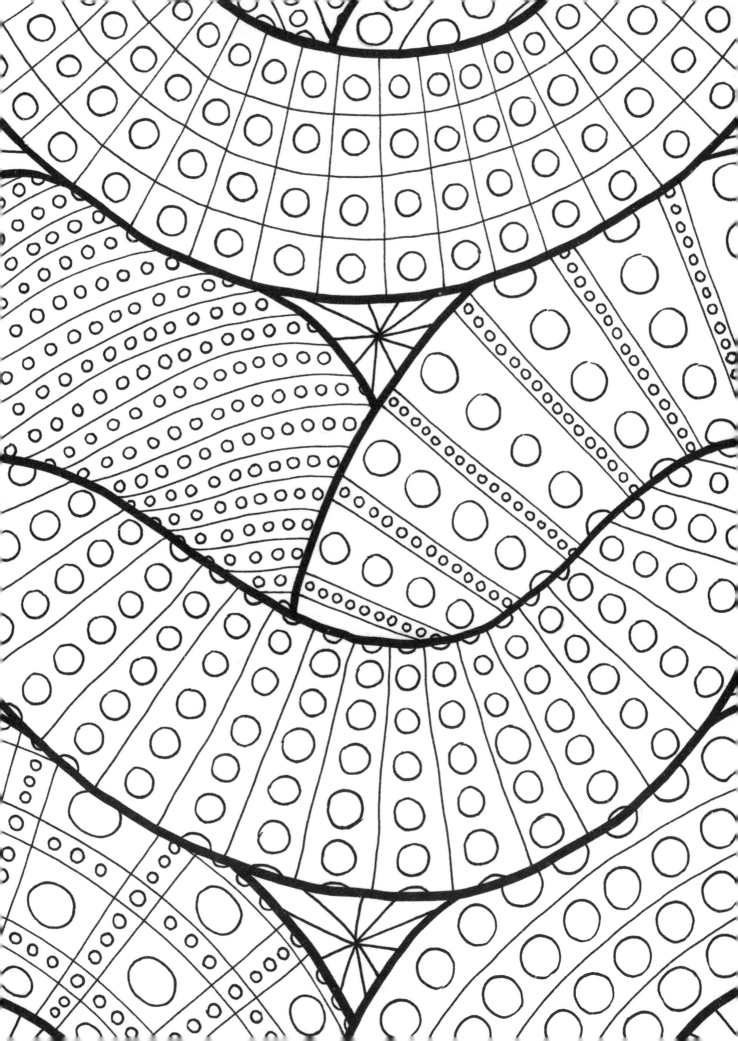

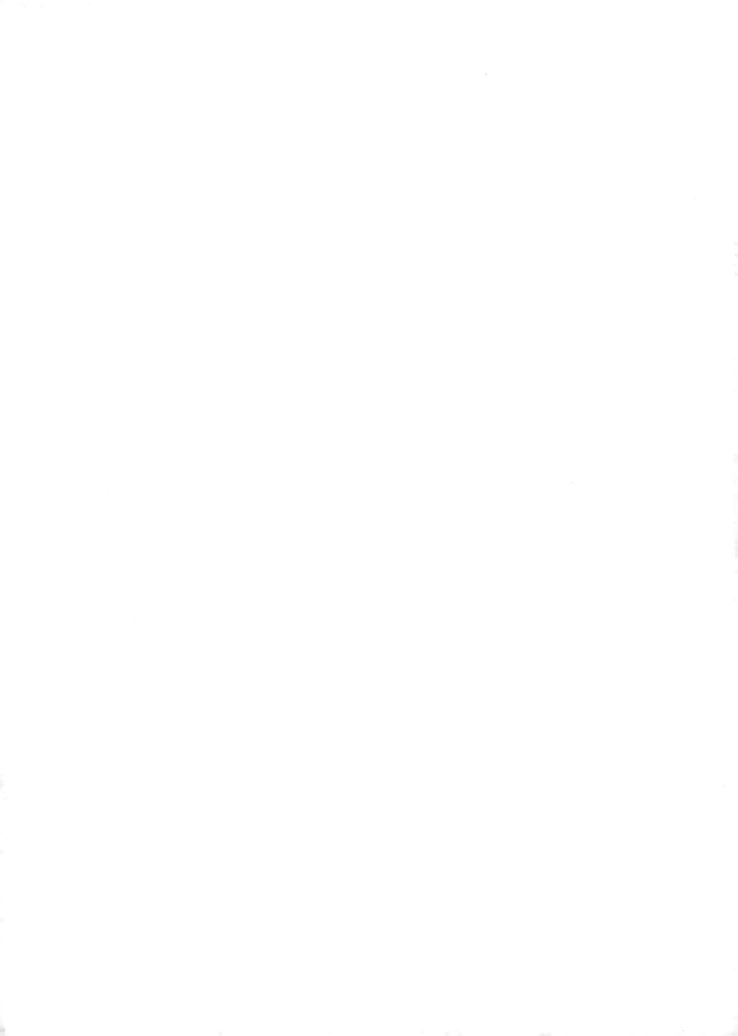

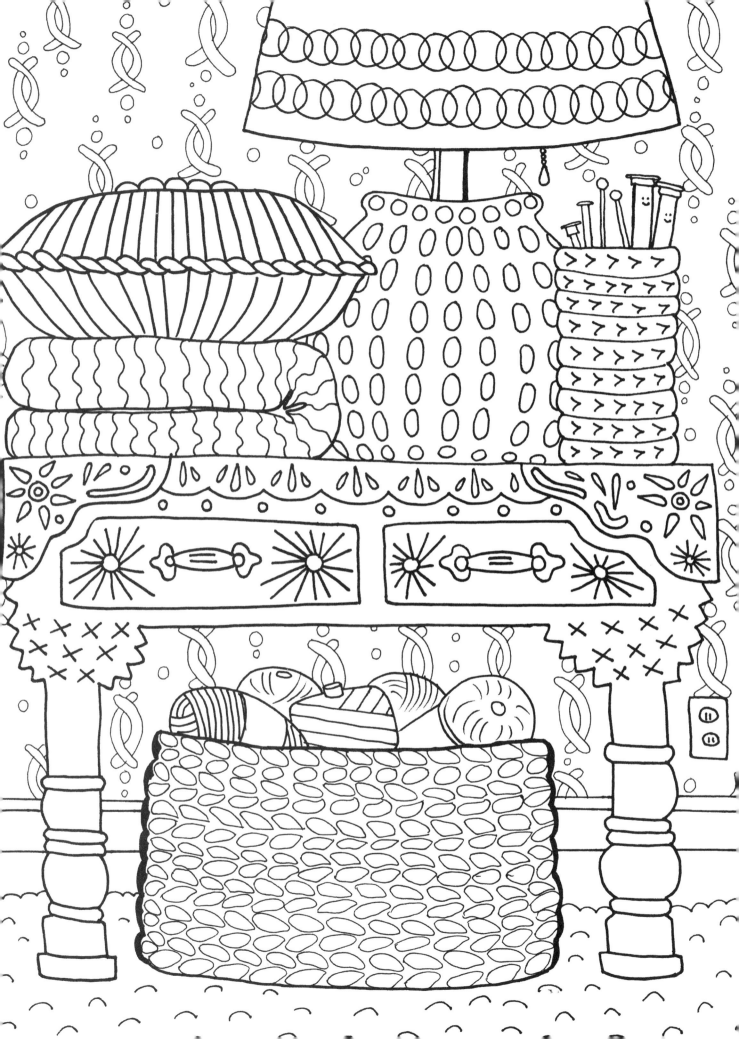

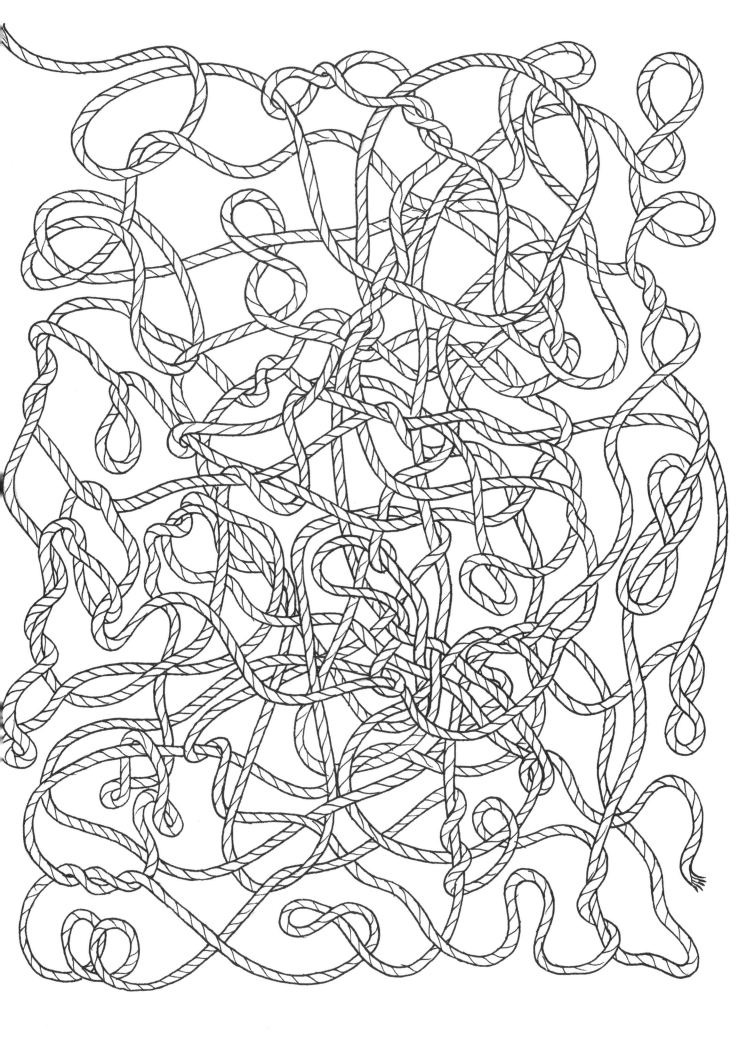

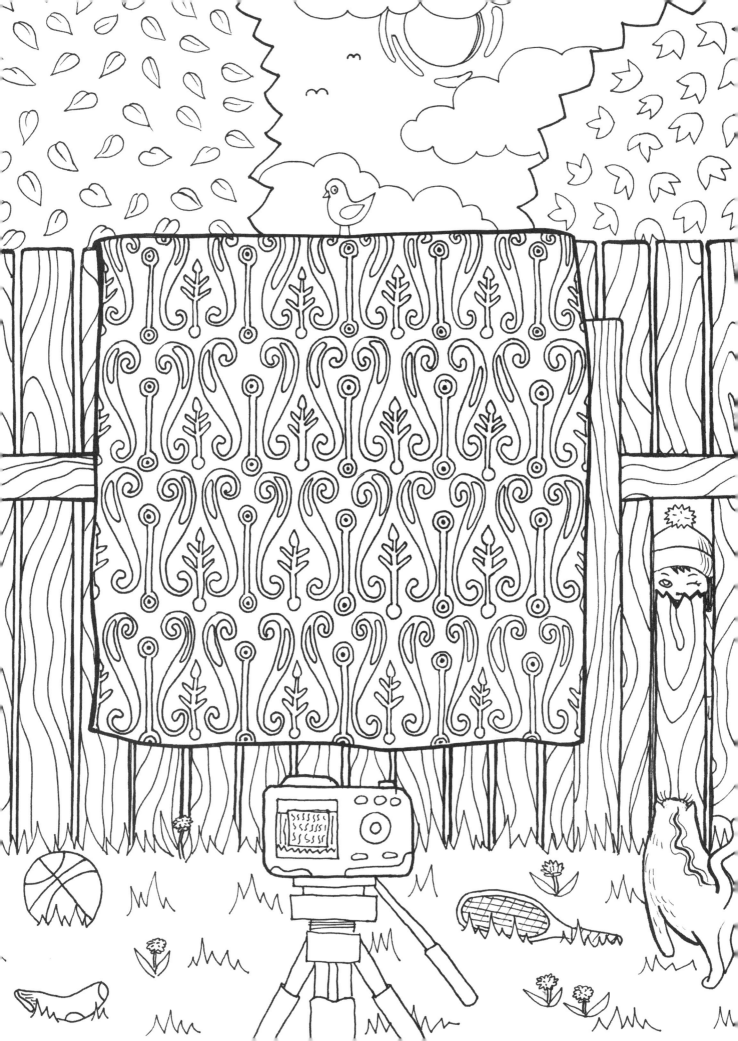

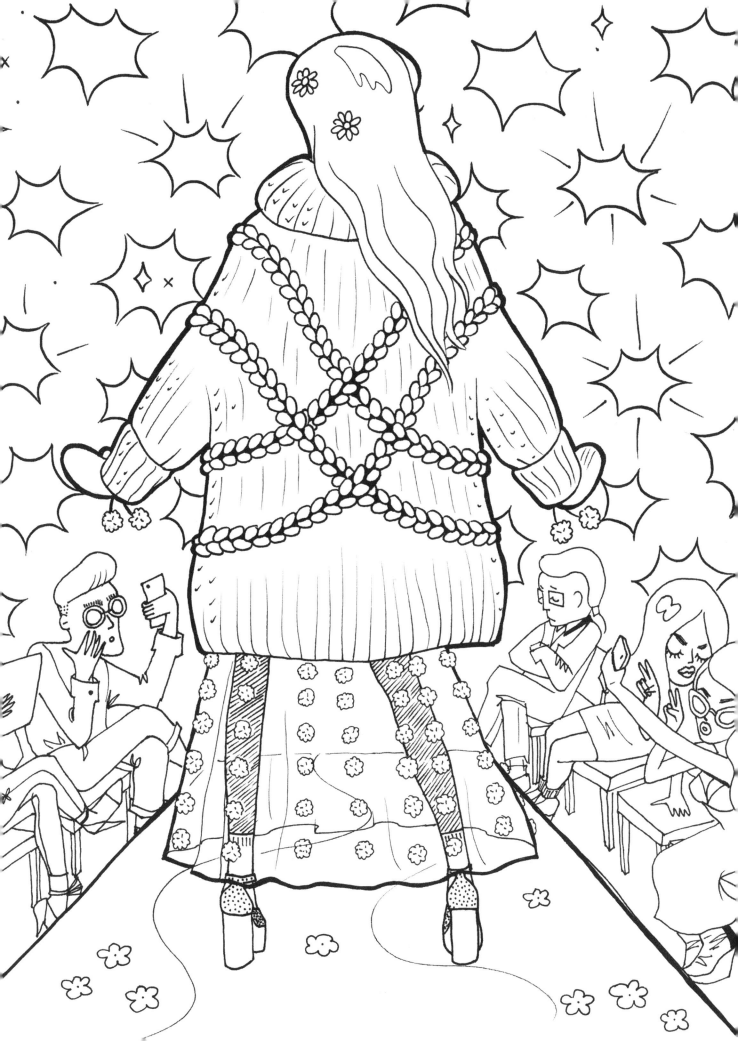

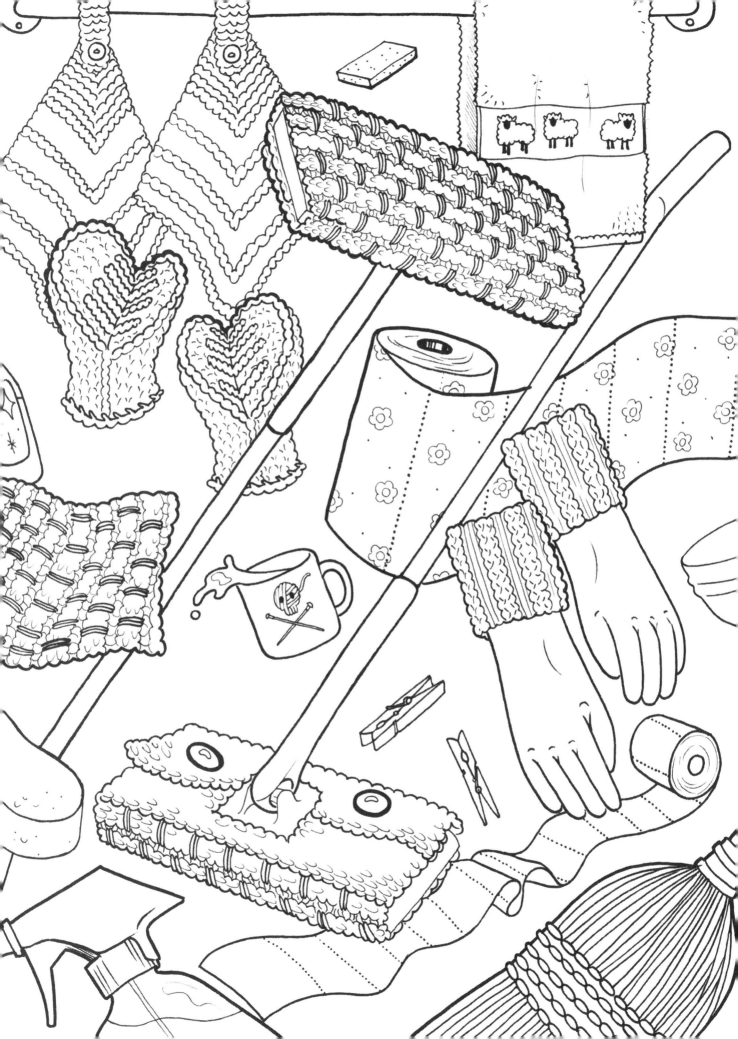

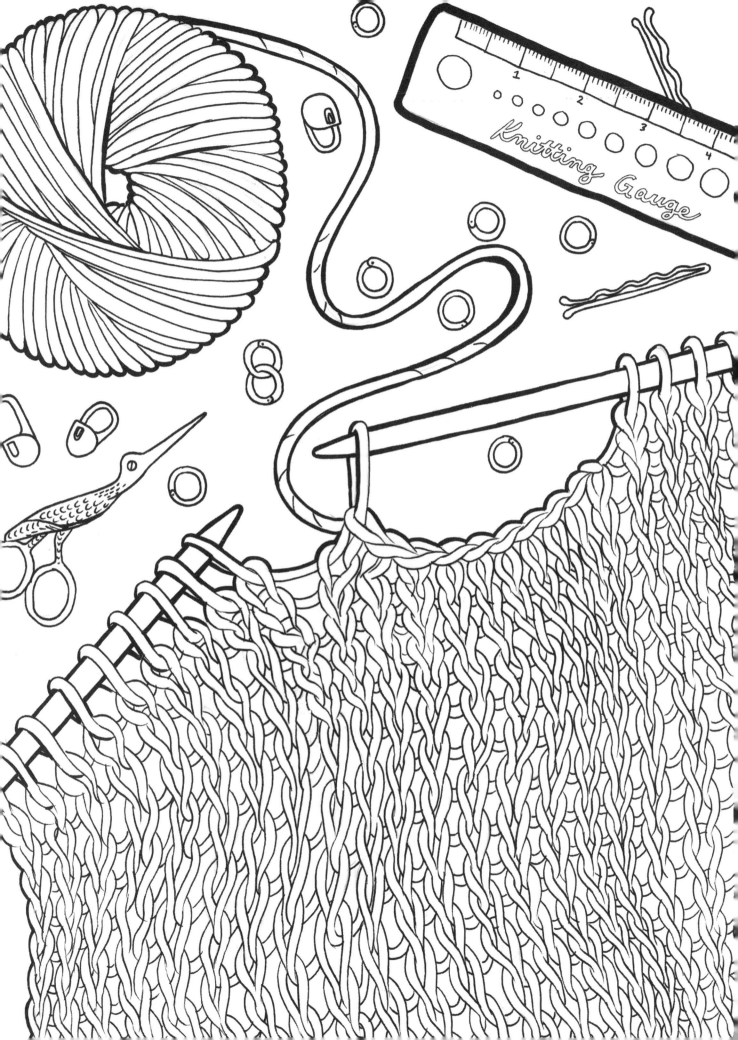

Knitting Gauge

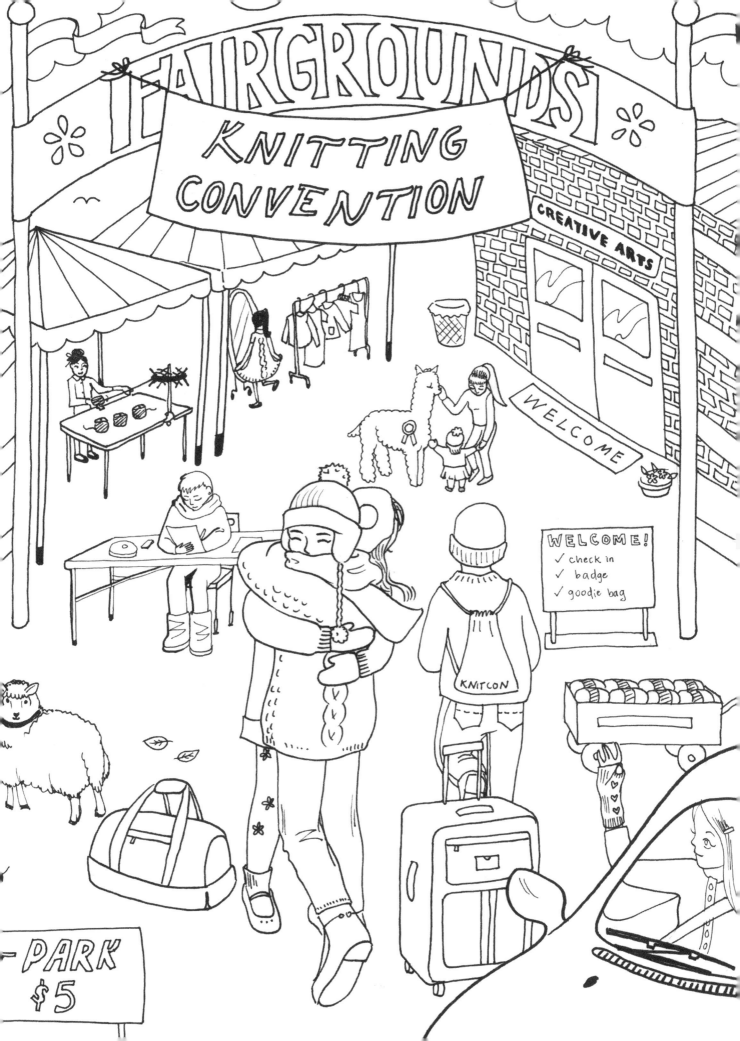

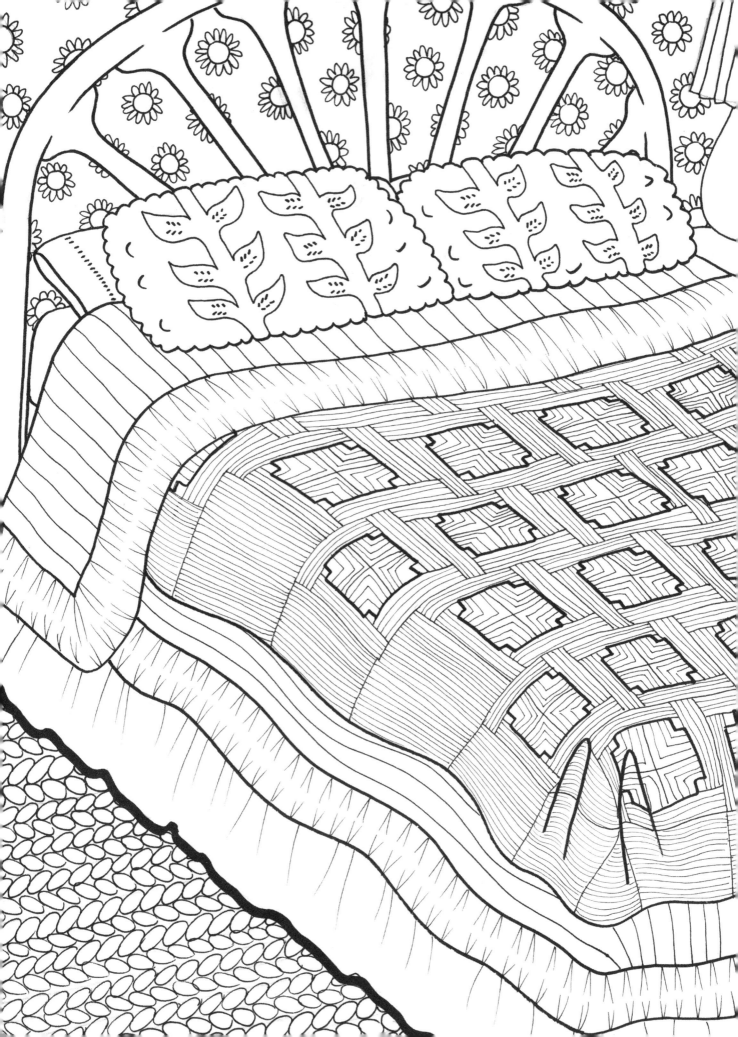

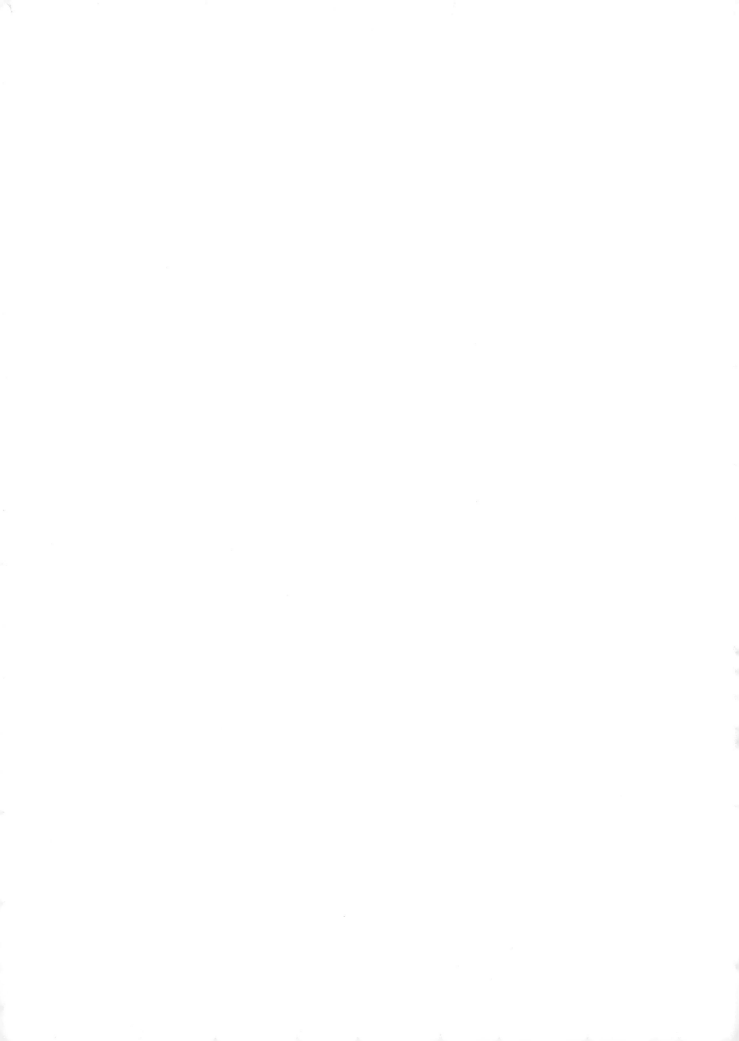

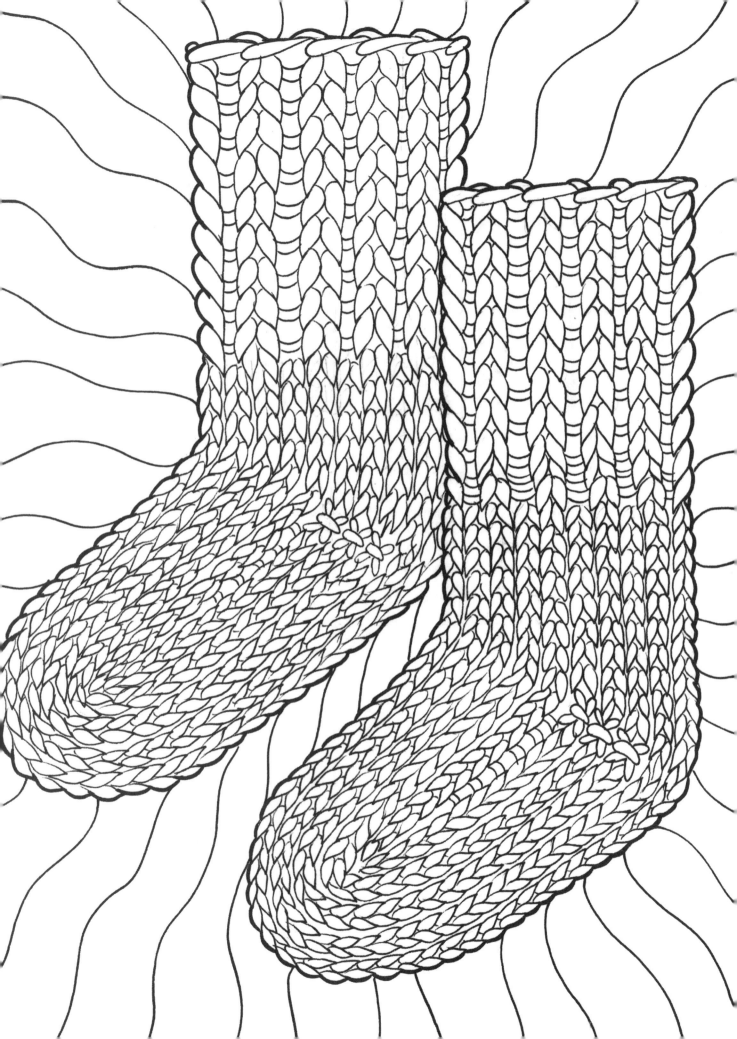

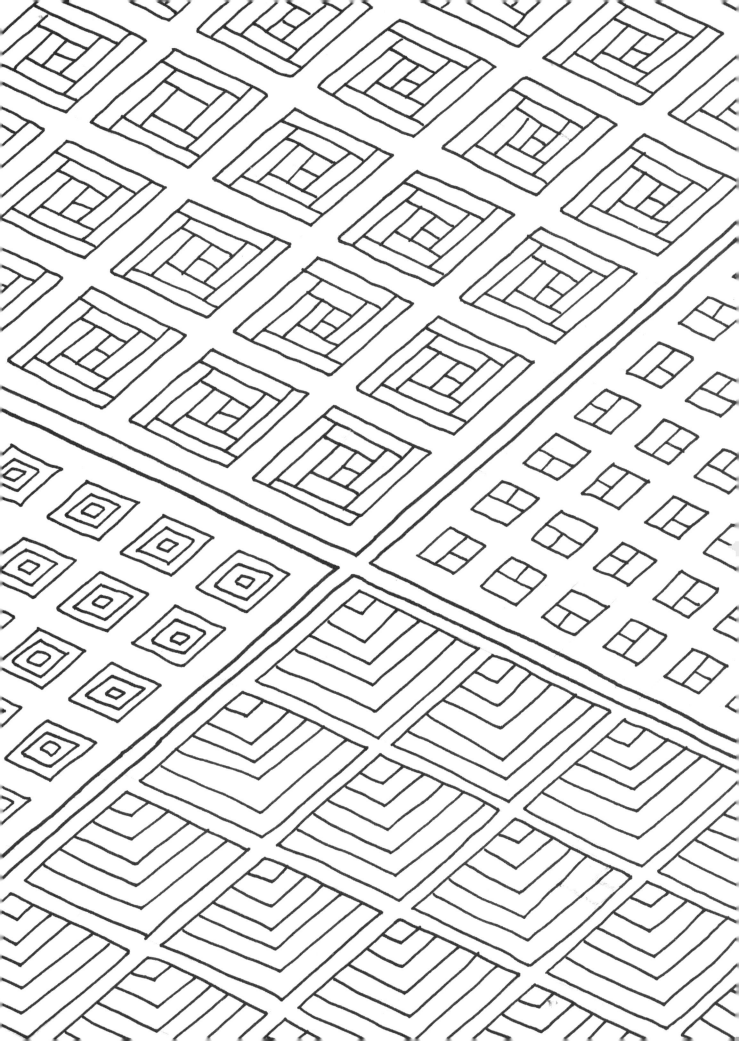

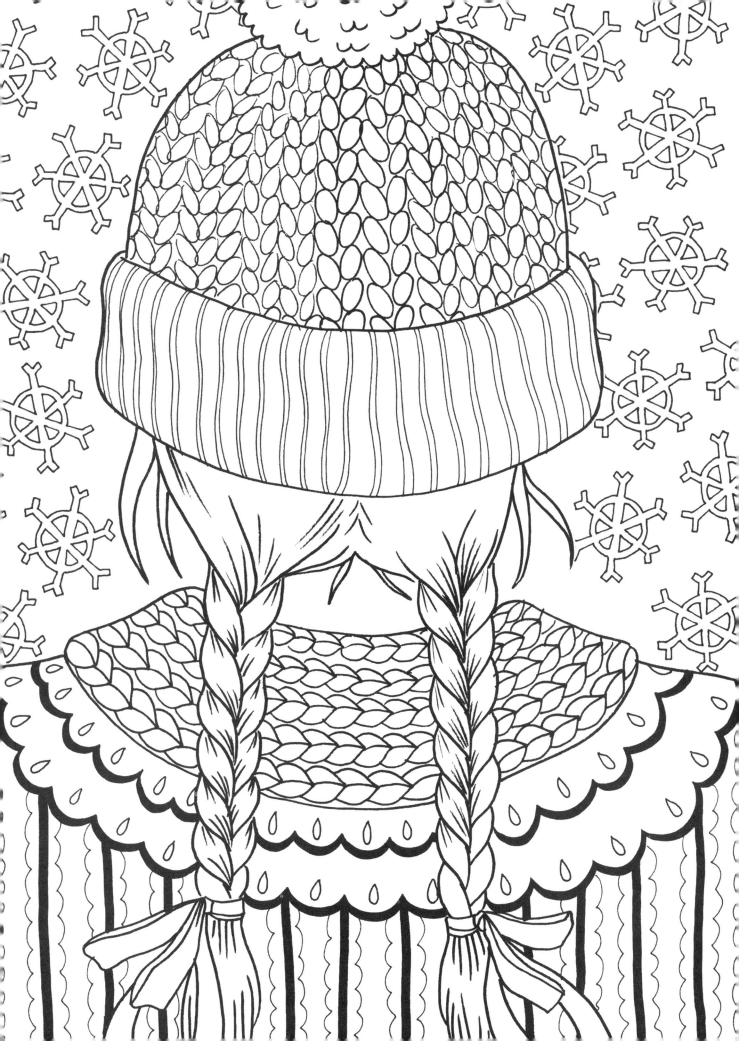

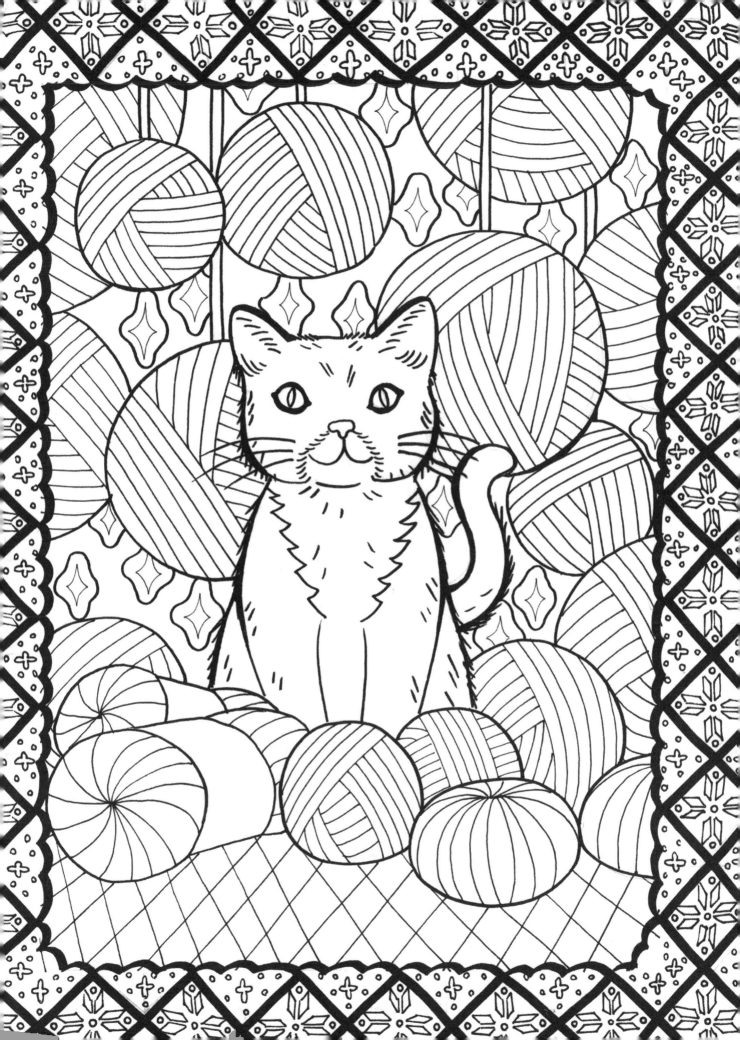

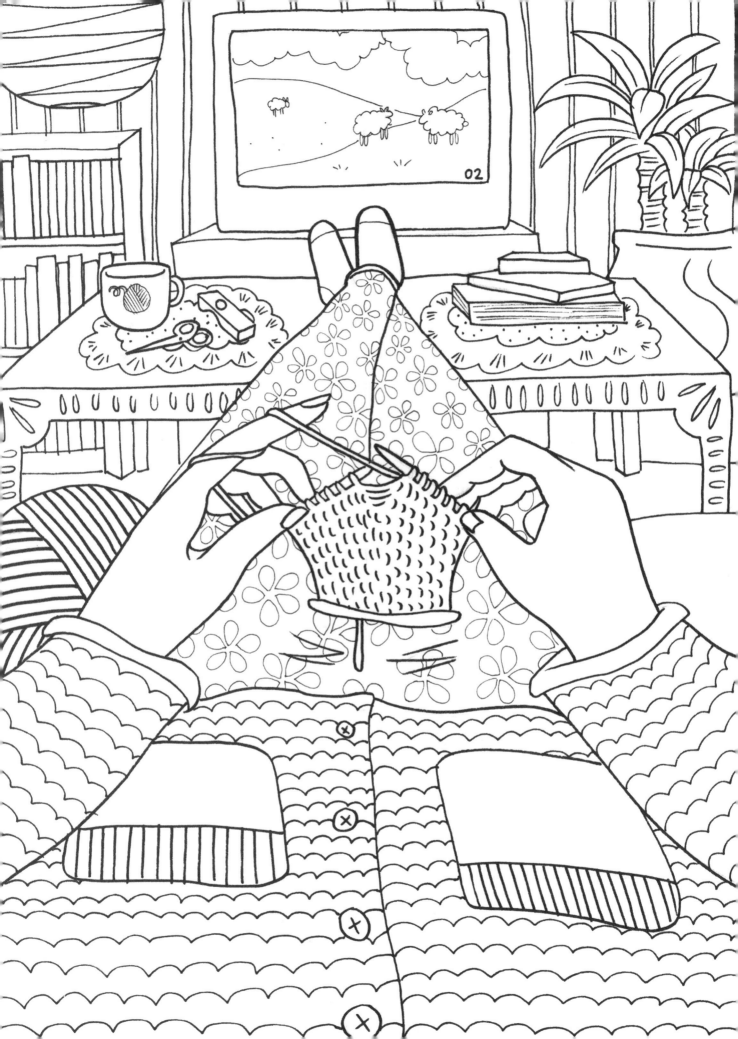

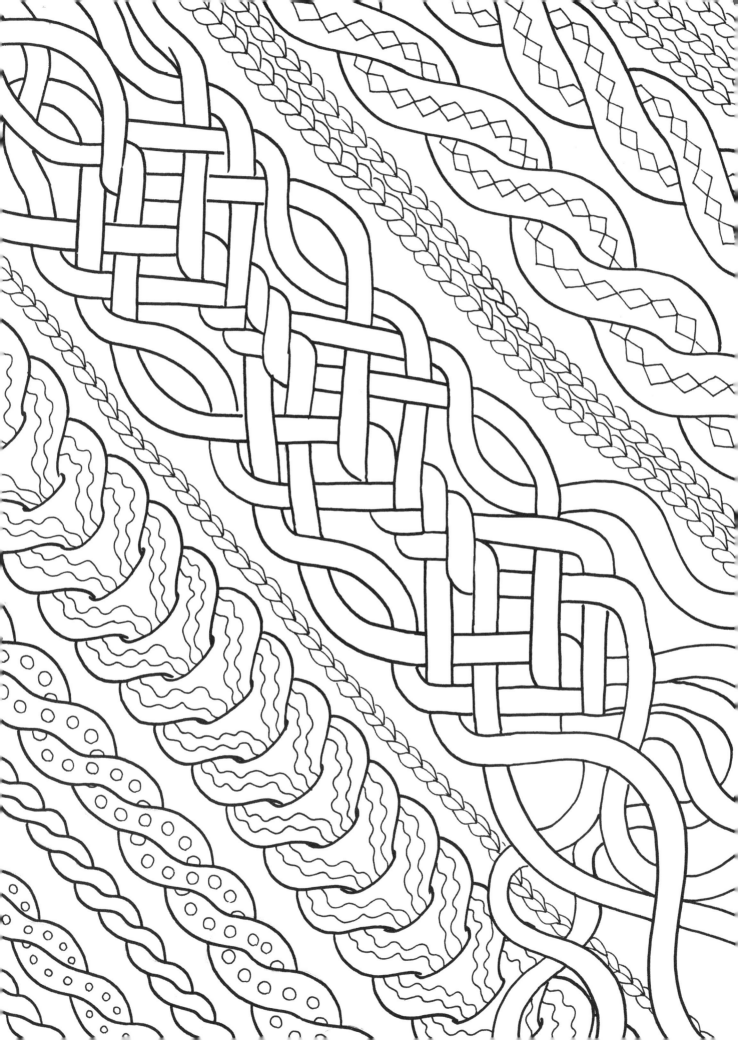

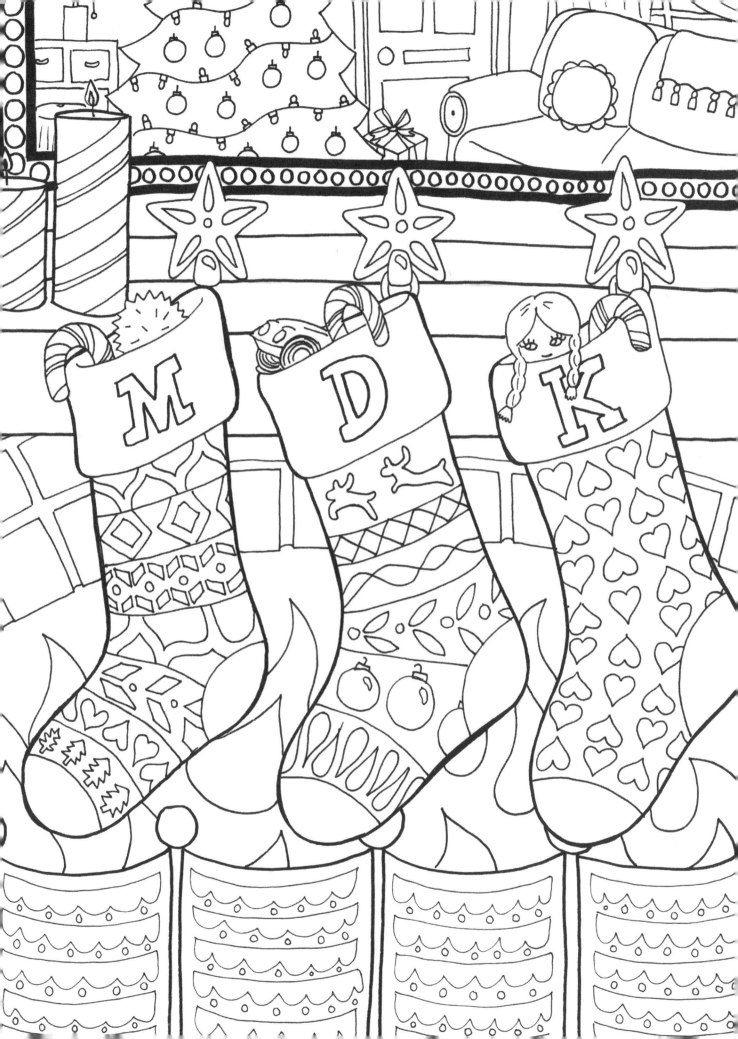

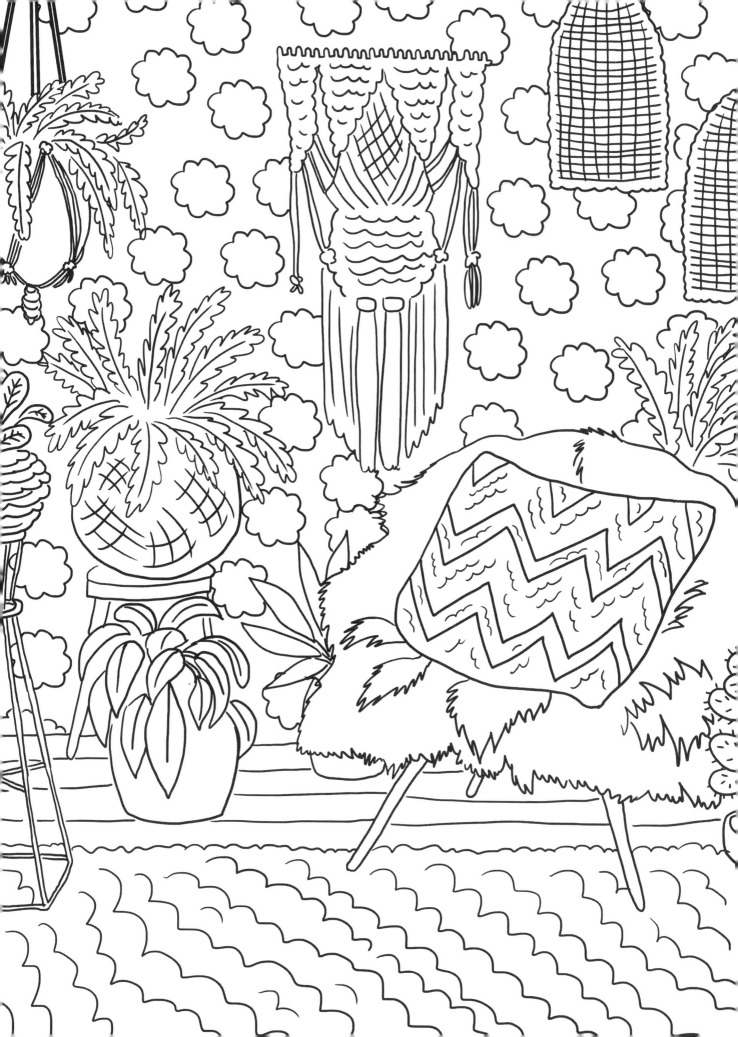

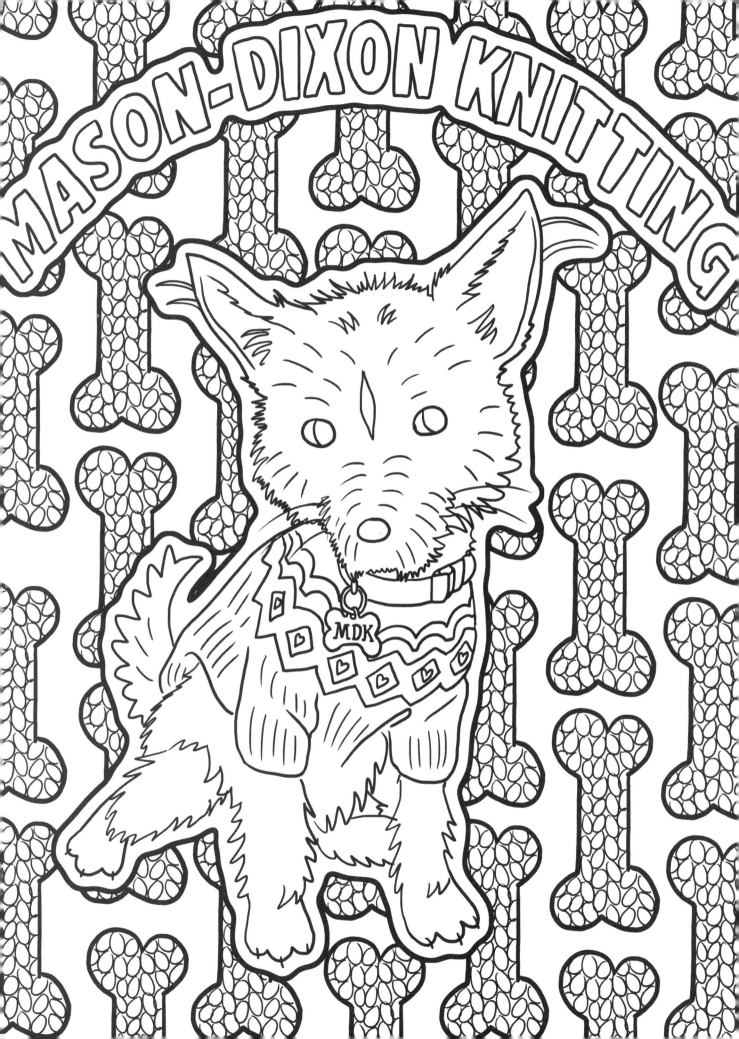

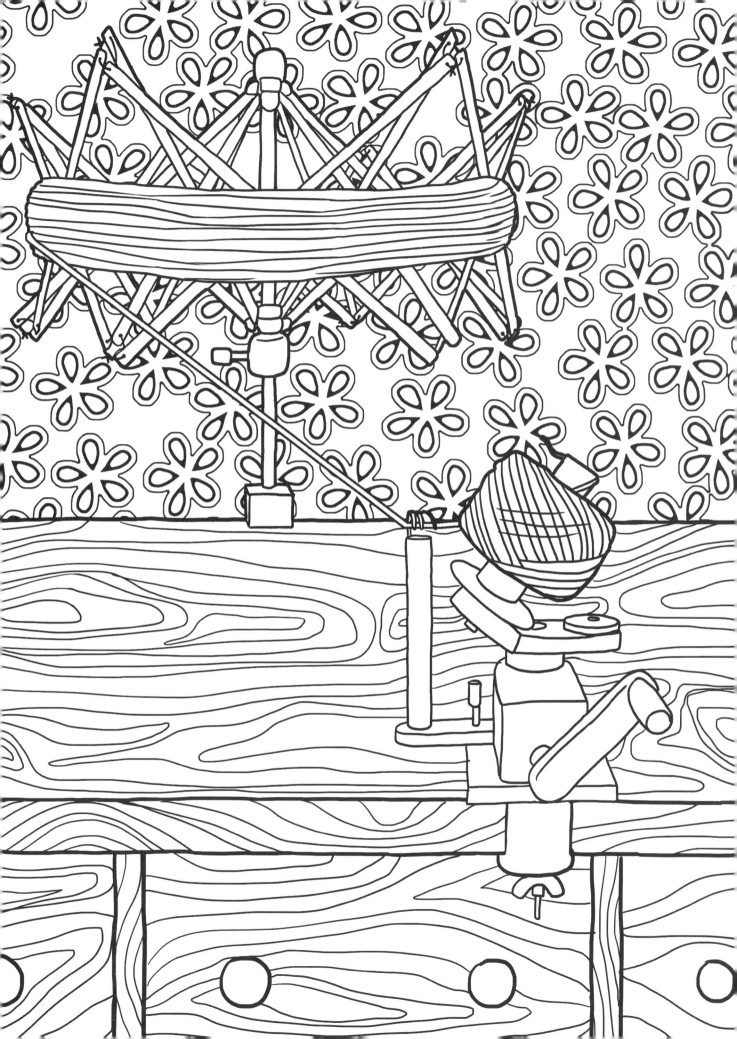